It's a gas!

BY **Margaret Griffin**
AND **Ruth Griffin**

ILLUSTRATED BY Pat Cupples

Kids Can Press Ltd. • Toronto

Kids Can Press Ltd. acknowledges with appreciation the assistance of the Canada Council and the Ontario Arts Council in the production of this book.

Canadian Cataloguing in Publication Data

Griffin, Margaret, 1948-
    It's a gas!

Includes index.
ISBN 1-55074-120-9

1. Gases - Juvenile literature. I. Griffin, Ruth,
1915- . II. Cupples, Patricia. III. Title.

QC161.2.G75 1993   j533   C92-094397-7

Kids Can Press Ltd.
29 Birch Avenue
Toronto, Ontario, Canada
M4V 1E2

Edited by Valerie Wyatt
Designed by Michael Solomon
Printed and bound in Canada by Metropole Litho Inc.
93 0 9 8 7 6 5 4 3 2

TABLE OF CONTENTS

ACKNOWLEDGEMENTS

From the very beginning, writing *It's a Gas!* has been a family project. Three generations and several branches of the family collaborated on this book across an international border. We would like to thank all the children and grandchildren, parents, sisters, brothers, cousins and in-laws who helped, collectively as well as individually. Thanks! It was a lot of fun.

Once again, we'd like to thank Alexander and Dinah Weldon (Margaret's children and Ruth's grandchildren). They cheerfully tested activities and performed experiments on demand, often for a second or third time. Fourth-graders at the Willingdon School in Montreal also tried many of the experiments and read parts of the text. We would like to thank all of them as well as their teachers, Ingrid Karbin and K.E. Cumming. We're also grateful to Barbara Weiss for curing Alexander's hiccups.

We'd also like to thank Dominique Young, author of *Explore and Discover*, and Steve Rosenstein of the Nomad Scientists in Montreal. Deborah Seed, co-author of *The Amazing Egg Book*, deserves a special thank you for her continuing friendship and support.

Katherine Reed M.D. (McGill University Student Health Service, Montreal, Quebec) and Peter H. Scott M.D. (Scottish Rite Children's Medical Center, Atlanta, Georgia) both read the manuscript with safety issues in mind. We very much appreciate their valuable advice.

We'd like to thank the entire team at Kids Can Press — thanks to Lori Burwash and the production crew; Louise Oborne, the copy editor; Pat Cupples, the illustrator; Michael Solomon, the designer; and especially Val Wyatt, our editor.

Much of the research for this book was done in the Resource Centre of Champlain College, St. Lambert, Quebec. We would like to thank the librarians there for their interest and assistance.

Last but not least, John Weldon must be thanked for all the times he came to our rescue at the computer.

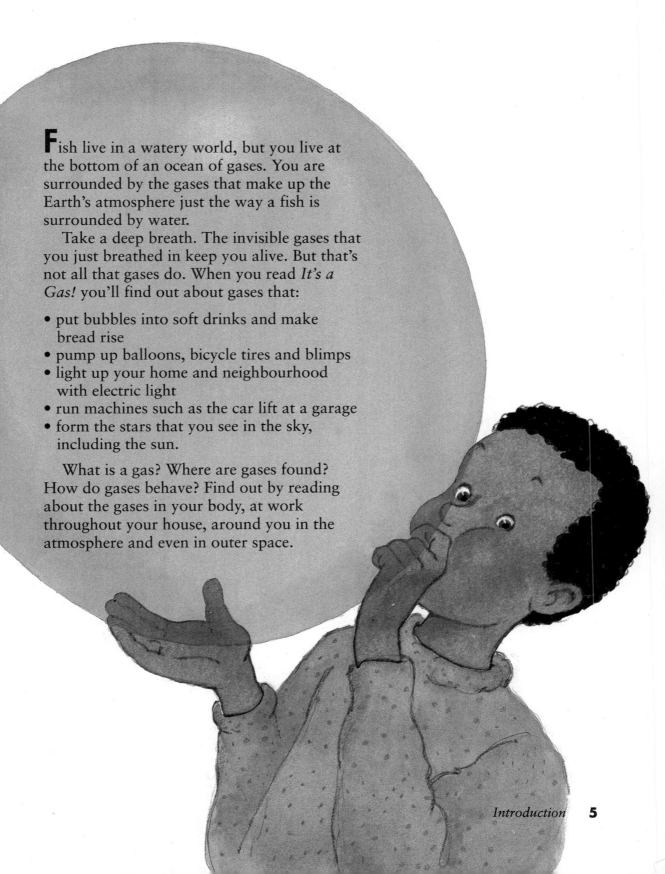

Fish live in a watery world, but you live at the bottom of an ocean of gases. You are surrounded by the gases that make up the Earth's atmosphere just the way a fish is surrounded by water.

Take a deep breath. The invisible gases that you just breathed in keep you alive. But that's not all that gases do. When you read *It's a Gas!* you'll find out about gases that:

- put bubbles into soft drinks and make bread rise
- pump up balloons, bicycle tires and blimps
- light up your home and neighbourhood with electric light
- run machines such as the car lift at a garage
- form the stars that you see in the sky, including the sun.

What is a gas? Where are gases found? How do gases behave? Find out by reading about the gases in your body, at work throughout your house, around you in the atmosphere and even in outer space.

How gases behave

Put an ice cube on a plate in front of you and think for a minute about what you see. Ice is a solid. It has a definite shape of its own. Let the ice cube sit out for an hour. It will change from a solid to a liquid, and it won't be a cube any more. Liquids take the shape of whatever container they are in. Now put the plate of water in a warm place for a day or two. The water will change shape again, this time into an invisible gas, part of the air around you.

Although you cannot always see, feel or smell gases, they are real things. Gases are composed of atoms and molecules just as liquids and solids are.

Gases are made of molecules just like liquids and solids.

DID YOU KNOW?
An empty 1-L (1-quart) milk carton sitting out on the kitchen counter contains about 27 000 000 000 000 000 000 000 molecules of gas. Can you picture that many things fitting into such a small space? Now try to imagine all those molecules hurtling around at the speed of sound, about 1200 km/hr (750 miles per hour). At least a billion collisions take place between molecules in that carton every second. And you thought it was empty!

SOLIDS, LIQUIDS AND GASES

Why are water, ice and steam different? They're all made up of water molecules, but water molecules that behave in different ways. Molecules are always in motion. In solids, liquids and gases, molecules move in different ways.

• In a solid, the molecules are linked tightly together in an orderly pattern. They can't move around freely. They just vibrate, or shake, in the same spot.

• In a liquid, the molecules shake hard enough to break out of their fixed positions in the pattern. They move around loosely in an unorganized crowd, jostling and bumping into one another all the time. Molecules in a liquid move faster than the molecules in a solid.

• In a gas, the molecules are moving very fast, even faster than the molecules in a liquid. The molecules spread out, far apart from one another. In a gas, the spaces between the molecules are enormous compared to the size of the molecules themselves.

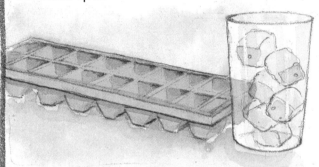

Is this space taken?

Here's a trick that will prove to your friends that an empty bottle isn't empty — it's filled with gases.

You'll need:
• a balloon
• a plastic soft-drink bottle
• an elastic band

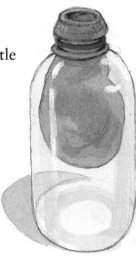

1. Push a balloon down into the neck of a soft-drink bottle, turning the open end of the balloon down around the rim as shown. Secure the balloon in place with the elastic band.

2. Ask your friend to blow up the balloon. It's impossible! Your friend can't force much air into the balloon because the space between the balloon and the walls of the bottle is already filled with air. The air he's trying to blow in has no place to go.

Gases occupy space.

Can you tell what's for dinner as soon as you walk in the front door? Something yummy? Or . . . oh no, not leftovers from last night!

Fortunately, not all smells are bad. Think of the wonderful smell that you experience when you break open an orange. An orange peel is the original scratch-and-sniff. Manufactured scratch-and-sniffs borrow nature's great idea.

How do scratch-and-sniff products work? Take a look at one under a magnifying glass. (Perfume samples in magazines work well.) You should be able to see tiny bubbles. They're filled with a strong-smelling liquid, which is sealed in by the bubbles' protective shells. When you scratch the surface, the shells break open. The smelly liquid evaporates into a gas that travels rapidly through the air to your nose.

In the same way that a smell can quickly fill up a room or a house, a gas expands to fill all the space available. A gas will spread out evenly to fill any size container — a milk bottle, a garbage can, a room, a house. A gas can fill the whole world! Just think — the oxygen molecules you're breathing in right now may have been inhaled before by someone walking on the Great Wall of China.

> Gases spread out to fill the space they're in completely.

Why do onions make you cry? When you slice one open, molecules from the onion are carried away by the gases in the air, spreading out into the room. The onion molecules that reach your face combine with the water in your eyes to produce a form of sulphuric

SOB!

acid. Owww! Some cooks recommend refrigerating the onion before slicing it, or rinsing it under water as you work. Other people suggest holding a piece of bread between your teeth. The bread sticks out and stops the onion fumes before they can reach your eyes.

Weighing two gases

Helium-filled balloons float because helium is lighter than air. Other gases are heavier than air. Here is an experiment to compare air and carbon dioxide gas.

You'll need:
- 7 mL (½ tbsp) baking soda
- a large plastic soft-drink bottle
- 45 mL (3 tbsp) vinegar
- a small piece of cardboard
- a wooden metre stick or yardstick
- 2 plastic foam cups
- a pencil
- a shoebox

1. Put the baking soda into the bottom of a clean plastic soft-drink bottle, then pour the vinegar in all at once. Quickly cover the top of the bottle with the palm of your hand. (Wet your hand first to make a better seal.) When the bubbling stops, gently remove your hand and quickly cover the mouth of the bottle with a piece of cardboard.

2. Build a simple scale as shown. It doesn't have to balance perfectly. Just make sure that the cups have stopped moving and that the measuring stick is not touching the shoebox.

(If one cup is lower than the other, choose it to fill up in step 3.)

Gases have mass just like solids and liquids.

Some gases weigh more than others.

3. Slowly and carefully pour the carbon dioxide gas (but none of the liquid) out of the soft-drink bottle and into one of the cups. Be very careful not to bump the balance or the table. Watch what happens as the cup fills up with carbon dioxide. Why does the cup sink down?

4. Check the balance again in 15 or 20 minutes. What do you think has happened?

WEIGHING IN

The Earth's atmosphere weighs some five million billion kilograms (about ten million billion pounds) because each atom of gas has a very tiny but definite mass. Although you can't feel it, air is pressing down on you right now. There is about 1 kg of air pressing down on every square centimetre of your skin (or 15 pounds on every square inch). If you could squeeze all the air in your classroom into a suitcase, you wouldn't be able to move it; it would weigh about 100 kg (220 pounds).

Bouncing bubbles

You can use carbon dioxide gas instead of air to blow some extraordinary soap bubbles. If the carbon dioxide gas is inside the bubbles, they won't be much fun. They'll fall to the ground and pop even faster than ordinary bubbles. So try this instead — use carbon dioxide gas *outside* the bubbles! The result? Bubbles that seem lighter than air.

You'll need:
- 125 mL (½ cup) baking soda
- 750 mL (3 cups) vinegar
- a large plastic picnic cooler with a lid
- bubble-blowing solution
- a bubble blower

1. An hour ahead of time, prepare a large amount of carbon dioxide gas. To do this, pour the vinegar into the picnic cooler and sprinkle the baking soda over the vinegar. Put the cover on quickly, and leave the closed container undisturbed until all signs of bubbling and fizzing have stopped.

2. Remove the lid from the cooler. Kneel at one end of the cooler and blow bubbles across the opening. Watch what happens to the bubbles that start to drift down into the cooler. When they reach the layer of carbon dioxide gas that has settled in the bottom, they'll bounce back up, hovering over the layer of carbon dioxide. If they don't hit the sides of the cooler and break, these air-filled bubbles will float over the carbon dioxide. Why? The air inside these bubbles is lighter than the carbon dioxide.

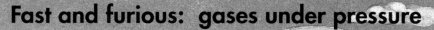

Fast and furious: gases under pressure

Can you describe the difference between an empty balloon and an inflated one? What keeps a blown-up balloon fat and round? And what makes it pop if you blow it up too much? The molecules of air inside the balloon are moving very fast, knocking into each other and forcing each other apart. Those molecules are also colliding with the walls of the balloon, pushing outward. As you blow more and more air into the balloon, you increase the number of molecules inside, the number of collisions — and the pressure. The skin of the balloon is stretchy. It grows bigger, but thinner, as the pressure builds up inside. Eventually, the skin gets so thin that — POW! — a molecule crashing into it bursts right through.

Gases can be compressed.

• Gases can be compressed, or squeezed, into liquids. If enough gas is forced into a small space, the molecules are squashed so close together that they start to behave like the molecules in a liquid.

• Natural gas is compressed into a liquid and bottled for easy shipping and storing; 645 L of natural gas are compressed into a single 1-L tank of liquified natural gas.

Turning up the heat

The pressure of a gas in a container depends on the size of the space and the number of molecules inside. Heat is another thing that puts the pressure on. Why? As a gas is heated, the molecules speed up. Even if the number of molecules stays the same, they crash into each other more and more often — and hit with more and more force. Try this experiment to see how heat increases the pressure of a gas.

You'll need:
• an empty plastic soft-drink bottle
• sand or rice to weigh the bottle down
• a large bowl
• hot tap water
• a coin large enough to cover the mouth of the bottle
• a freezer

1. Put several handfuls of sand or rice in the bottle. It must be heavy enough to stand in a bowl of water without floating or tipping over.

2. Place the bottle in the freezer long enough to be sure that the gases inside the bottle are really cold. This will take a couple of hours.

3. When you're ready to do the trick, ask an adult to place the bottle in the large bowl filled with very hot tap water. If the bottle floats, add more sand or rice.

4. Wet the lip of the bottle and cover the opening completely with the coin. In several minutes, the coin will start to click up and down on the bottle. (Be patient. It may take longer than you think.) Why does the coin move? As the gases inside the bottle warm up, the pressure builds until it is great enough to lift up the coin. Some of the expanding gases escape. The pressure falls as air rushes out, letting the coin drop down again temporarily. The coin will continue to jump as long as the water is hot enough to keep warming the gases in the bottle.

When gases cool down, the moving molecules slow down and the pressure that they exert drops, too. Gases shrink, or contract, as they cool. Measure around the biggest part of a blown-up balloon, then put the balloon in the freezer for several hours. Measure it again. Is it any smaller?

INSTANT ENERGY

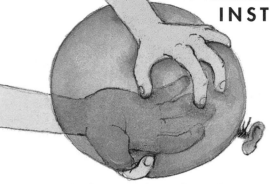

Blow up a balloon until it's about three-quarters full. Squeeze it gently between the palms of your hands. Can you feel the air inside pushing back? Squeeze harder and the pressure pushing your hands apart will also be stronger. Compressed gases exert pressure, too.

Blow up a balloon but don't tie it closed. Hold the neck of the balloon between your thumb and forefinger and then let go. Where did that balloon get enough energy to go flying around the room? The energy was held by the gases inside the balloon. Both the energy and the gases were just waiting for the chance to escape.

When you blow up a balloon, you are compressing gases. Lungfuls of air are squeezed into a much smaller space. Because the molecules of a gas are very far apart to begin with, they can be forced closer together. But a gas under pressure will expand again as soon as it has the chance. This makes compressed gases a useful way to store energy or exert force.

You can see — and hear — compressed gases at work at a gas station. When a car is put on a lift, compressed air does the lifting.

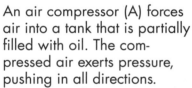

An air compressor (A) forces air into a tank that is partially filled with oil. The compressed air exerts pressure, pushing in all directions.

When the compressed air pushes *down* on the surface of the oil in the tank (B), the oil pushes *up* on the piston in the smaller cylinder of the lift (C), lifting your car.

When it's time to bring the car down again, a valve is opened to release the compressed air. Listen for the hiss of the escaping air as the lift is lowered.

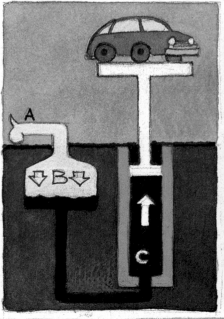

Taking a dive

Some toys also use compressed gases. Here's one that you can build yourself. It's called a Cartesian diver.

You'll need:
- the cap from a large marker
- a hammer
- a nail
- a waterproof felt pen
- paper clips
- a plastic soft-drink bottle
- water

1. Ask an adult to help you make two holes at opposite sides of the marker cap. This can be done with the hammer and nail.

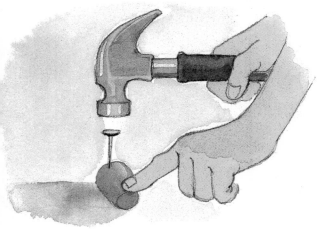

2. Draw a face on the cap, using the waterproof felt pen. This is your diver.

3. Hang a chain of three paper clips from each hole.

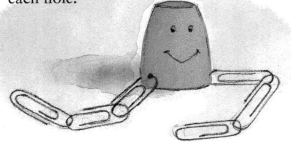

4. Fill the soft-drink bottle three-quarters full with water and drop the weighted cap inside. It should float just below the surface of the water. If the diver sinks too low in the water, remove one paper clip from each chain and try it again. If the diver floats on the water's surface, add an extra paper clip to each chain.

5. Screw the cap tightly onto the bottle.

6. Squeeze the bottle firmly, using both hands. In a moment, the diver should descend gently towards the bottom. When you stop squeezing, the diver will float back up towards the surface again.

The diver was floating just below the surface of the water because of the bubble of air inside the marker cap. Why does it start to sink when you squeeze on the bottle? Squeezing the bottle compresses the air both inside the bottle *and* inside the diver. There's more water inside the diver now, making it heavier; it can't float as high in the water and sinks. When you stop squeezing, the bubble of air inside the cap expands again, forcing the extra water out. This makes the diver lighter again, allowing it to rise.

A matter of life and death: dissolving gases

Have you ever tasted a glass of water that's sat out in the open too long? It tastes pretty weird. Why? All the gases that are usually dissolved in the water have escaped, making the water taste "flat." If you don't like drinking flat water, imagine what it must be like to be a fish living in a flat pond. For the fish, it's not just a question of a bad taste; it's a matter of life and death. If there is not enough oxygen dissolved in the water, a fish will not be able to breathe.

Many fish have gills that remove the oxygen from the water in much the same way your lungs remove oxygen from the air. A fish takes water in through its mouth and forces it out through the gill slits on the sides of its head. As the water passes over the gills, it drops off its load of oxygen.

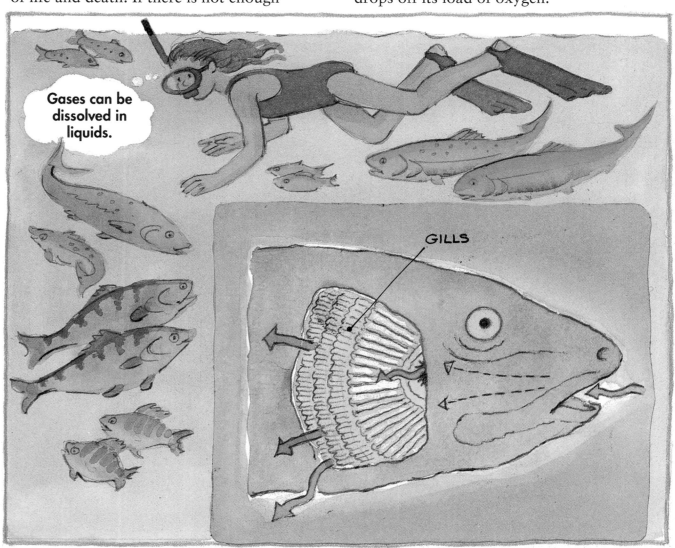

Crystal clear

You can't see the gases that are dissolved in ordinary tap water. Or can you? Turn that ordinary tap water into an ordinary ice cube and take another look. The bubbles and tunnels you see in the ice were made by trapped gases. The more gases there were dissolved in the liquid water, the cloudier the ice cube will be.

Why are most of the bubbles found in the centre of an ice cube? When you put an ice-cube tray of water into the freezer, the cold reaches the surface of the water first. The water freezes from the top down and from the edges in, pushing the gases ahead as it goes. The bubbles are trapped in the centre of the block as the water freezes.

If you want to make some very clear ice, here's how to do it. If it's winter, you may want to make windows for a snow fort this way.

You'll need:
- plastic foam trays (vegetable trays work better than meat trays because they're deeper)
- boiled, cooled water
- a freezer

1. Fill a plastic foam tray with water that has been boiled and allowed to cool. Boiling will have driven off most of the gases that were dissolved in the water.

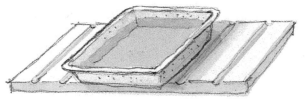

2. Place the tray in the coldest part of the freezer, making sure that it is level.

3. Check your pane of ice in several hours. You'll want to remove it before it is completely frozen, while it is crystal clear. All the gases are still dissolved in the unfrozen water at the bottom of the tray.

DID YOU KNOW?

In the summer, some fish go into estivation. That's the hot-weather equivalent of hibernation, the sluggish state that some animals go into during the winter. Why do fish have to slow down when hot weather comes? Warm water can't hold as much oxygen as cool water can. When the weather and the water heat up, the fish cope with the oxygen shortage by becoming inactive.

Less gas can be dissolved in a warm liquid than in a cool one.

Gases in your body

When you were born, your lungs filled with air for the very first time, and you started to breathe. For the rest of your life, you will have to take another breath every few seconds just to stay alive. You might be able to live for several weeks without food or for a few days without water. But without oxygen, one of the gases in the air, you couldn't survive for more than a few minutes.

Your body can store extra food as fat to use later on, but it cannot store very much oxygen. A continuous supply of fresh oxygen must be delivered to every cell day in and day out. That's where breathing comes in. Each breath delivers oxygen gas to your body and carries another gas, carbon dioxide, away. Carbon dioxide is made in abundance by each one of your millions of cells. It is a waste gas, one that your body must get rid of.

Some animals have special organs where this exchange of gases takes place.

• Large land animals like you have lungs to get oxygen from the air.

• Fish use gills to get oxygen from the water.

• Air enters a grasshopper's body through a row of small holes, called spiracles, in its abdomen.

• Other animals, such as jellyfish or earthworms, have no special apparatus for breathing. They absorb the oxygen they need directly through their skin.

SPIRACLES

I breathe with gills when I'm young, with lungs when I'm older and through my skin during hibernation. Who am I?

Answer on page 62.

Molecules on the move

To see how molecules can pass through a thin wall, such as the skin of a worm, try this.

You'll need:
- white writing paper
- water
- iodine (available at a drugstore)
- newspaper
- a plastic sandwich bag
- an elastic band
- a bowl

1. Wet a piece of white writing paper with water and put a drop of iodine onto it. Do the same thing with a piece of newspaper. The iodine changes colour when it comes in contact with starch. Writing paper is coated with a starchy mixture to make it smooth, so the iodine changes from brown to dark blue. Newspaper has not been starched, so the colour of the iodine stays the same. Now you're ready to see how molecules can move through a thin skin or membrane.

2. Pour 125 mL (½ cup) of water into the bag and test it for leaks. Once you're sure the bag isn't leaking, add a few drops of iodine to the water in the bag. Twist the bag closed and secure it tightly with the elastic band.

3. Set the bag into the bowl and almost fill the bowl with water. Hang a strip of white writing paper over the edge of the bowl as shown. Within an hour, a blue colour should start to appear on the paper strip just above the level of the water. Iodine and starch must have met. But how? Since the bag doesn't leak, molecules of iodine must have passed through the wall of the bag, through the water and onto the paper strip. In much the same way, molecules of air can pass through the skin of a worm.

What happens to the air you breathe once it flows into your lungs? Inside these spongy organs, the passageway leading from your throat divides again and again into thousands of microscopic branches. At the end of each branch is a cluster of air sacs, bulging out like a bunch of grapes. Gases can pass through the very thin walls of the air sacs into, or out of, tiny blood vessels called capillaries. In this way, gases such as oxygen and carbon dioxide can move back and forth between the lungs and the bloodstream.

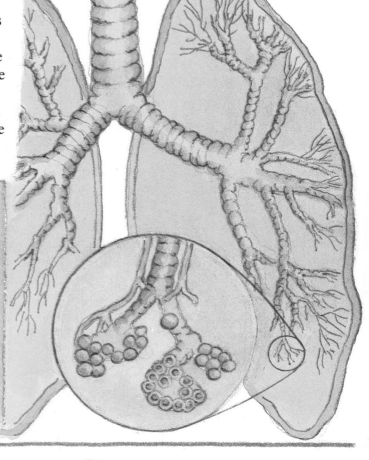

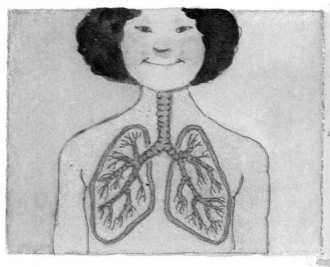

DID YOU KNOW?

An unborn baby uses oxygen carried through the bloodstream of its mother. The mother's capillaries and the baby's capillaries lie very close together, side by side. Although the two blood supplies never mix, molecules of oxygen and carbon dioxide pass freely back and forth.

In your blood

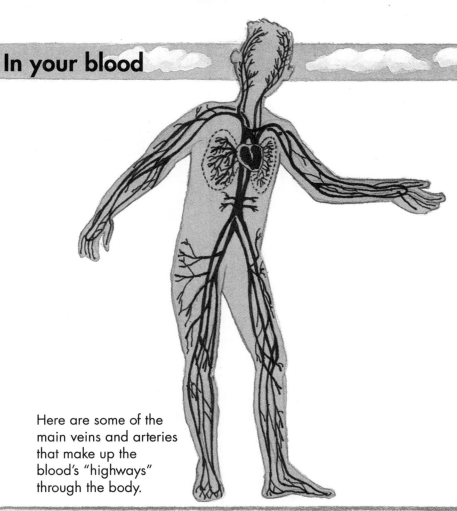

Here are some of the main veins and arteries that make up the blood's "highways" through the body.

What happens to the oxygen once it has passed into your blood? The oxygen is picked up and carried by your red blood cells as they are swept along in the liquid part of your blood. The red blood cells are filled with haemoglobin. This important chemical actively gathers up oxygen in the lungs, where it is plentiful, and releases it again when the blood reaches the cells where oxygen is needed. Haemoglobin makes it possible for the blood to carry about 40 times more oxygen than it otherwise could.

INSIDE A DROP OF BLOOD

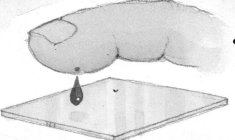

More than half (55 per cent) of each drop of blood is plasma, a thin yellowish liquid. The rest includes different types of blood cells carried along in the plasma.

A single drop of blood contains all these things, floating around in the plasma.

- 5 000 000 red blood cells that transport oxygen to your cells and carry carbon dioxide away
- 5000 white blood cells that help defend your body against invading bacteria or germs
  - platelets that help your blood clot when you cut yourself
- hormones that are your body's chemical messengers
- food molecules that are the food supply for your cells

In your cells

Why is oxygen so important to us? Oxygen can combine easily with many other chemicals, releasing energy as it does so. If you've ever seen a fire burning, you've seen this kind of process in action. A log burns when molecules in the wood combine with the oxygen in the air. A lot of energy in the form of light and heat is produced.

A slower form of oxidation takes place inside your body all the time. The oxygen that

is delivered to your cells is used to release the energy stored in the food you eat. Your cells "burn" food as a fuel. In your body, special chemicals called enzymes make it possible for this "burning" to take place slowly without producing too much heat. Some heat is produced — enough to keep your temperature around 37°C (98.6°F) — but most of the energy is chemical energy, the kind of energy that your body needs to make it go. Your cells keep their cool *and* get their work done.

MOUNTAIN SICKNESS

People who live high in the mountains are used to breathing air containing much less oxygen than the air at lower altitudes. Their bodies have adapted to thinner high-altitude air. They have larger lungs than you do, and almost one-third more red blood cells to transport oxygen to their cells. You could become used to the thinness of the air, too, but it would take time. When athletes went to compete in the 1968 Olympics in Mexico City, which is 2240 m (7350 feet) above sea level, they had to go through a special training period to get used to the thin air.

Mountain climbers who venture up more than 6096 m (20 000 feet) above sea level need to take an oxygen supply along

with them. Without extra oxygen, they would have to stop for a rest after every ten steps or so. Weakness is not the only symptom of altitude sickness, however. Other dangers include mental confusion, convulsions, unconsciousness and death.

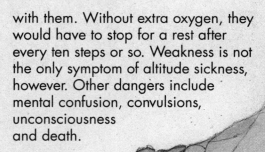

MORNING BREATH

Tomorrow morning, before you even sit up in bed, count the number of breaths that you take in a minute. Better yet, have someone else count your breaths while you're still asleep by watching your chest rise and fall. When you're resting and relaxed, your lungs and heart don't have to work very hard because your body isn't using up much energy. First thing in the morning you're probably breathing more slowly than at any other time of the day. Measure your breathing rate again while you sit quietly at the breakfast table. Has it already started to speed up as you begin another busy day?

The ins and outs of breathing

You breathe in oxygen and breathe out carbon dioxide, but that's only part of the story. The air you inhale is a mixture of gases, and so is the air you exhale.

NITROGEN

OXYGEN

CARBON DIOXIDE

Most of the air around you is nitrogen, a gas your respiratory system doesn't even use. Nitrogen makes up almost 80 per cent of each lungful you breathe in, but it's exhaled again, unused and unchanged.

The essential ingredient you need — oxygen — makes up a little more than 20 per cent of each breath of air. Only a small part of that is absorbed into the blood. There's still lots of oxygen in the air you breathe out — about 16 per cent of exhaled air is oxygen. That's why you can use the air you exhale to give artificial respiration to someone who has stopped breathing. You give him or her your leftover oxygen.

A tiny amount of carbon dioxide is present in the air you inhale, about $\frac{3}{100}$ of a per cent. When you exhale, you increase the amount of carbon dioxide gas more than 100 times, but the total amount still adds up to only about four per cent. So most of the air you exhale turns out not to be carbon dioxide after all.

TAKE A DEEP BREATH!

1. Stand up straight with your feet slightly apart. Stretch your hands out in front of you with your palms together.

2. Take a slow, deep breath. As you inhale, move your arms outward in a big circle, ending up with your hands clasped behind your back.

3. Tip your chin upwards and bend backwards as far as you comfortably can. Gently push your arms out from your body and up towards your head.

4. Now it's time to exhale. Slowly bend forward as you breathe out, letting your head drop. Keeping your knees straight, let your head hang as close to your knees as you can. Your arms stay in the same position as they were in step 3.

5. Straighten up slowly to a standing position and relax.

Have you ever found yourself panting for breath? Strenuous exercise, such as running, can make you need to breathe two or three times as fast as you normally do — and more deeply, too. Those extra, bigger breaths provide the extra oxygen you need and get rid of the extra carbon dioxide your body produces.

Part of an athlete's training involves learning to improve and control her breathing. Here's a tip that can help you next time you want to run, swim or skate hard. Take a couple of extra-deep breaths before you start. Try to fill and empty your lungs as completely as possible each time. When you're breathing normally, you usually don't bother to empty out your lungs more than halfway before you inhale some fresh air. Emptying your lungs as much as possible makes more room for fresh air — and the extra oxygen that it carries.

Emotions such as fear, anger or excitement can make you breathe faster, too. Slowing down your breathing rate, on the other hand, can help you relax. Here's a soothing breathing exercise to try. (And it's also a very good cure for hiccups.)

Carbon dioxide isn't the only gas your body has to get rid of. It also has to dispose of the gases formed in your stomach and intestines as you digest your food. These gases aren't exhaled. They come out as rude noises.

A burp, or belch, is the sound made by stomach gases erupting through your mouth. You burp when you swallow too much air with your food, or when you consume too much carbon dioxide in a soft drink.

Flatulence is produced in your intestines and is released through your anus. In addition to the gases found in ordinary air, flatulence contains hydrogen, methane (also called swamp gas) and hydrogen sulphide, which is the same compound that's responsible for the smell of rotten eggs. Bacterial action and the fermentation of food in your digestive tract produce as much as 10 L (2.6 U.S. gallons) of these gases each day. Fortunately, most of the gas is reabsorbed by your body as it passes through your intestines. Usually, only about 0.5 L (2 cups) of gas escape in the form of flatulence each day.

DID YOU KNOW?

The sound of your knuckles cracking may be the sound of gas bubbles popping. A liquid surrounds the joints in your fingers. Some scientists think that when you stretch your fingers, the pressure in the fluid is reduced and gases come out of solution with a tiny but audible pop!

Gases around the house

Living creatures aren't the only things that need gases. All sorts of household objects depend on gases, too. Look around your house, especially in the kitchen. Many of the things you see couldn't work without gases.

Lighten up: gases and lighting

Without gases, you'd be sitting in the dark. Why? Both ordinary light bulbs and fluorescent lights use gases. Here's how they work.

Most household light bulbs are incandescent bulbs. Electricity passes through the wire, or filament, inside the bulb, making it heat up enough to start to glow and give off light. You can feel the heat if you bring your hand near an incandescent bulb while it's on. How hot does a light bulb's filament get? Would you believe 2500°C (about 4500°F)? At that high temperature, the filament would burn up if any oxygen were in the air around it.

In the earliest light bulbs, the problem was solved by removing most of the air, leaving the filament in a vacuum. Today, modern bulbs are filled with an inert gas, a gas that will not react with the metal in the filament or allow it to burn. But the filament still disintegrates slowly over time. Do you know why old light bulbs turn grey? As the metal of the filament wears away, it covers the inside surface of the glass, darkening it.

SAY CHEESE!
Some bulbs are filled with oxygen gas so that the filament will burn out instantly. Can you guess what kind of bulbs have to burn out in a flash?

Fluorescent lights use gases, too. A small amount of mercury gas is sealed into a long glass tube, and an electrical current is passed through it. As moving electrons strike molecules of gas inside the tube, the mercury starts to give off rays of invisible ultraviolet light. The only problem is that you can't *see* ultraviolet light. Just as there are sounds that are too high for you to hear, there are types of light that are out of the range of human vision. Fortunately, when ultraviolet light falls on certain surfaces, it causes them to fluoresce (give off visible light). The light that you see shining from a fluorescent bulb actually comes from the layer of white phosphor that coats the inside of the tube and reacts with the ultraviolet light.

HAPPY BIRTHDAY GASES

Before you blow out the candles on your next birthday cake, take a closer look at this remarkable source of light.

What fuel does a candle burn? Is it the wax? The flame floats above both the pool of liquid wax and the solid wax of the candle itself. Neither is burning. Is it the wick? A string alone wouldn't burn like that. To see what is burning, ask an adult to help you with this experiment. Blow out a candle and ask the adult to immediately hold a lighted match in the smoke, about 1 cm (½ inch) above the wick. The candle will burst into flame again.

The match reignites the hot gases evaporating from the melted wax. It is the gaseous wax vapour that burns to make candlelight.

When you blow out a candle, you're cooling it off so much that combustion can no longer take place. Every fuel, including wax vapour, must reach a certain temperature before it can burn. It's not too much carbon dioxide or a lack of oxygen that makes the flame go out. In fact, there's enough oxygen in your breath to fan up a fire. That's why blowing on the coals of a dying campfire will revive it.

Place the bowl of a spoon on the palm of your hand and pour a few drops of room-temperature water into it. Does the spoon suddenly feel cooler? The water in the spoon cools off as it begins to evaporate (change into a gas). Why? Water molecules escaping from the liquid take a little bit of energy in the form of heat with them. Since the most energetic molecules tend to escape, the average energy of the remaining molecules is less, and the temperature falls.

For thousands of years, people who have lived in hot countries have known that evaporation can cool things. Drinking water can be kept cool in porous clay pots or thick canvas bags. As the water seeps slowly through the walls of the container and evaporates from the surface, the contents inside are cooled — but only slightly. Modern refrigerators are a lot better — and a lot more complicated.

Would you believe that your refrigerator is really a heater in disguise? A refrigerator cools your food by taking heat away from the inside of the refrigerator and pumping it out into the room. Your kitchen gets hotter as your food gets colder.

How does your fridge move the heat from one place to another? It uses a gas. Let's take a trip around the inner workings of a fridge to find out how it works. A molecule of Freon has volunteered to be our guide. And what is Freon? It's a brand-name chemical that is used in many cooling systems because it changes easily from a gas to a liquid, and from a liquid to a gas.

My friends and I were down at the bottom of the fridge, hanging around the entrance to the compressor. Everything was cool. We were all spread out, running around and doing our own thing, when we heard footsteps coming into the kitchen. "Oh, no!" someone yelled. "It's that kid again! Everybody get ready!"

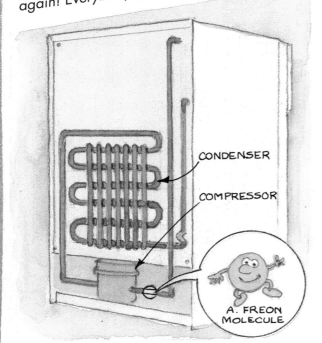

CONDENSER

COMPRESSOR

A. FREON MOLECULE

"Didn't his mother ever teach him not to stand around with the fridge door open?" I thought to myself. But it was too late. The door was wide open, and the temperature inside the refrigerator was rising fast.

A gas gets hotter when it is compressed.

EVAPORATOR TUBES

CONDENSER

COMPRESSOR

A. FREON MOLECULE

We heard the compressor motor suddenly turn on. We grabbed one another tightly as we were pulled into the compressor. Being compressed is no fun! I'd rather be a gas than a liquid, but right now we had no choice. We were being squeezed into a liquid.

"Hang on!" I cried. "Only another second and we'll be out of the compressor." Boy, were we hot.

A moment later we poured out of the compressor into the condenser. Phew! We had to zigzag back and forth across the back of the refrigerator like molecules running a marathon. At least we got a chance to cool off a bit. The condenser is the part of the tubing that you can see from the outside. It's usually on the back, and it's the part that feels warm. As we ran through this maze of tubing, we gave off a lot of heat into the room.

Just when I was beginning to think I couldn't run any farther, the tube turned suddenly. We were leaving the condenser and heading for the inside of the fridge. Through the crowd of other molecules, I tried to get a glimpse of the tiny hole that led into the evaporator. We were almost halfway home!

A liquid cools as it evaporates or expands.

We burst into the evaporator tubes. At last there was room to spread out. Molecules went flying apart in all directions. We would have been happy if we weren't so cold. Once we had expanded into a gas again, the temperature in the tube got colder and colder. I shouldn't complain though. It's all part of our job.

The tubes of the evaporator run through the fridge, inside the walls where you can't see them. Our job while we were in there was to mop up the heat that the kid had let into the fridge. Luckily, we warmed ourselves up in the process. By the time we left the evaporator and headed back to the compressor, we were all feeling pretty good.

"Keep your fingers crossed!" someone yelled. "Let's hope the kid has found what he wants."

But we weren't so lucky. We had to make another four or five trips before he finally closed the door and went away.

Gourmet gases

Has all this talk about refrigerators made you feel hungry? DON'T OPEN THAT REFRIGERATOR DOOR! Let those poor Freon molecules get some rest. Try out this experiment and some recipes instead. Cooking can be a real gas.

You'll need:
- 12 small plastic foam cups
- measuring spoons
- baking powder
- baking soda
- cream of tartar (available at a grocery store)
- citric acid (available at a drugstore)
- marking pen
- hot and cold water

1. Measure the ingredients listed below into six of the cups and label them carefully.

> Cup 1: 5 mL (1 tsp) baking powder
> Cup 2: 5 mL (1 tsp) baking soda
> Cup 3: 5 mL (1 tsp) cream of tartar
> Cup 4: 5 mL (1 tsp) citric acid
> Cup 5: 2 mL (½ tsp) baking soda and 1 mL (¼ tsp) cream of tartar mixed together
> Cup 6: 2 mL (½ tsp) baking soda and 1 mL (¼ tsp) citric acid mixed together

2. Make a second set of cups with the same ingredients and label them clearly.

3. Add 15 mL (1 tbsp) of cold water to each cup in the first set. Do some of the mixtures start to bubble sooner than the others? Do some of them keep bubbling longer? What about the size of the bubbles?

4. Try the experiment again, adding hot water instead of cold to each cup in the second set. Do you notice any differences?

The chemicals you've been experimenting with are often used in cooking. The bubbles of gas they produce make soft drinks fizz, breads rise and cakes light and airy. The gas is carbon dioxide. Look carefully at a slice of cake before you eat it. Those little round air pockets show where bubbles of carbon dioxide gas formed in the batter.

Some of the simplest recipes for muffins, cakes and cookies use plain baking soda to make carbon dioxide gas. Are you surprised? The cup containing baking soda on its own (Cup 2) did not produce any bubbles when you added cold water to it. And it only produced a few when you added hot water. You have to add something else in addition to water to make the baking soda really start bubbling. That "something else" is acid. Vinegar works because it's a mild acid. Cooks also use lemon juice, yogurt or molasses because all of these things are slightly acidic, too.

Mystery cake

Look carefully at the ingredients in this recipe. Can you figure out which ingredient provides the acid that helps this cake rise?

You'll need:
- 2-L (8-inch) square cake pan
- 2 medium-sized mixing bowls
- 500 mL (2 cups) oatmeal (not instant)
- 375 mL (1½ cups) chopped dates (try using scissors!)
- 250 mL (1 cup) butter
- 250 mL (1 cup) boiling water
- 2 eggs
- 250 mL (1 cup) brown sugar
- 250 mL (1 cup) chopped walnuts (optional)
- 2 mL (½ tsp) baking soda
- 125 mL (½ cup) flour
- 5 mL (1 tsp) cinnamon
- 5 mL (1 tsp) ground cloves

1. Ask an adult to preheat the oven to 350°F.
2. Lightly grease the cake pan.
3. Put the oatmeal, dates and butter in a medium-sized mixing bowl and have an adult add the boiling water. Stir until the butter is melted.
4. Mix in the eggs, brown sugar and chopped walnuts. Set this mixture aside to cool.
5. In another bowl, combine the rest of the ingredients.
6. Stir the wet mixture into the dry ingredients, mixing well.
7. Spoon the batter into the prepared pan and bake at 350°F for 60 minutes, or until a knife inserted into the centre of the cake comes out clean.

Get an adult to help you whenever you need to use the stove.

If you're having trouble spotting the acid in this list of ingredients, here's a clue: all fruits are at least mildly acidic. The fruit in this recipe is acidic, too. Yes, it's the dates that provide the acid needed to make this cake rise.

Pita pockets

Cakes, cookies and muffins are sometimes called quick breads. They're made with baking powder or baking soda, and the bubbles of carbon dioxide gas are produced as soon as the ingredients are mixed. These snacks are usually in and out of the oven in less than an hour. Homemade breads, on the other hand, take much more time to prepare.

The only thing quick about these pita breads will be how fast they disappear! Although they are also leavened by carbon dioxide, the gas is produced in a very different and much slower way. Tiny living organisms called yeasts produce the carbon dioxide gas as they digest the sugars in the other ingredients of the dough.

Try making this recipe on the weekend, when you'll be around the house most of the time. These pitas freeze well, so you'll be able to use them for school lunches all week long.

You'll need:
- 2 mixing bowls (one large and one small)
- 500 mL (2 cups) warm water
- 10 mL (2 tsp) honey
- 2 packages of granulated yeast
- 60 mL (¼ cup) olive oil
- 15 mL (1 tbsp) salt
- 1.25-1.4 mL (5-5½ cups) all-purpose flour
- butter
- a bread board
- a tea towel
- a rolling pin
- a cookie sheet

1. Put 125 mL (½ cup) of the warm water into a large bowl and stir in the honey. (Sprinkle a few drops onto your wrist and make sure it's warm, not hot. The water should not be *too* hot or it will kill the yeast.) Sprinkle the yeast over the surface of the water, then gently stir it in. Leave the bowl in a warm place for 10 to 15 minutes to activate the yeast. When you come back, the mixture should be bubbly.

2. In a small bowl, add the oil and salt to the other 375 mL (1½ cups) of warm water, then pour this mixture into the bowl with the yeast.

3. Start stirring in the flour, one cup at a time. When the dough gets too stiff to stir, turn it out onto a floured board and knead more flour in. Keep kneading the dough for ten minutes, adding enough flour to keep it from sticking to the board.

4. Wash out the mixing bowl you mixed the dough in and dry it. Rub some butter all over the inside of the bowl. Roll the ball of dough around in the bowl until it's well coated with butter. Cover the dough in the bowl with a clean, damp towel and leave it in a warm place for several hours until it has doubled in size.

5. Wash your hands. When the dough has risen, plunge one of your fists into the middle of the swollen ball to deflate it. All that extra air is carbon dioxide gas released by the yeast. Turn the dough back out onto the floured board and knead it a few times. Can you hear the gas escaping? Cover the dough with the towel again and let it rest for 10 or 15 minutes.

6. Divide the dough into ten pieces and shape them into balls. Cover them and leave them for another half an hour.

7. Roll the balls of dough out into very thin circles. (Two circles should just fill a cookie sheet.) Now — you guessed it! — you'll have to wait some more. Cover the dough for another half an hour and ask an adult to preheat your oven to 500°F.

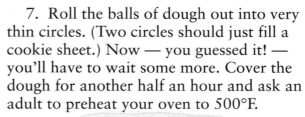

8. Ask an adult to bake the pitas two at a time on a cookie sheet placed on the middle shelf of the oven. Each batch will take about ten minutes to cook. When the pitas come out of the oven, the hot gases inside will have inflated them like balloons. They'll deflate into nice flat pitas as they cool. Cover the pitas with a clean dish towel as they cool to keep them from drying out, then store them in plastic bags.

Kitchen helpers: other gases in the kitchen

Carbon dioxide gas deserves the credit for giving us soft drinks and baked goods, but other gases have jobs to do in the kitchen, too. Because it is inert, nitrogen gas is often used to package perishable foods such as coffee or bacon. (Any contact with oxygen in the air would make these products spoil more quickly.) Chlorine gas is used to bleach flour and turn it white. Many cooking fats, such as margarines and shortenings, are prepared by bubbling hydrogen gas through a liquid oil to convert it into a solid fat. This process is called hydrogenation. Sulphur dioxide gas is used to preserve dried fruits such as apricots and raisins.

Gases can be used to stop fruits from ripening or to make them ripen faster. Apples are refrigerated and stored in an atmosphere rich in carbon dioxide gas to prevent them from ripening and spoiling too fast. On the other hand, ethylene gas is used to speed up the ripening of some types of fruits, including tomatoes, kiwis and bananas. These fruits can be picked while they're unripe and not too delicate for shipping. At their final destination, they are put in a container of ethylene gas and allowed to ripen.

Go bananas

You can ripen fruit with ethylene gas for yourself at home. Where will you get the ethylene? In this activity, the fruits produce it themselves!

You'll need:
- a bunch of ripe bananas (look for yellow and black skins)
- a bunch of unripe bananas (look for yellow and green skins)
- brown paper sandwich bags

1. Put one of the unripe bananas inside a paper bag. Fold the bag closed and set it aside. Let this banana ripen all by itself.

2. Put one unripe banana and one ripe banana into another paper bag. Fold the end closed tightly and put the bag in the same spot as the first bag.

3. Put one unripe banana and several ripe ones in a third bag. Close the bag and put it with the others.

4. Check the bananas in each bag every day. Which bananas ripen the fastest? Does the number of ripe bananas in the bag make a difference? If your bananas get too ripe, use them for making banana bread.

DID YOU KNOW?

Some trees can send messages to one another, and they use a gas to do it. Listen to this unusual murder mystery story. Scientists in South Africa were puzzled when hundreds of kudus (a kind of antelope) were dying during every dry season. It turned out that the kudus were being poisoned by acacia trees, one of the kudus' few sources of food.

As a kudu eats the leaves off one acacia, the tree starts to emit ethylene gas. When the neighbouring trees are exposed to the gas, they start to produce tannin, a poisonous and unpleasant-tasting chemical. Usually, the tannin discourages the kudu from eating any more acacia leaves. Unfortunately, when food is very scarce, kudus may be forced to eat enough acacia leaves to poison themselves.

COOKING WITH GAS

Do you have a gas stove in your kitchen? If you do, you're cooking with gas — natural gas. This fuel is a mixture of gases produced in a natural way. The gases form as dead plants and animals decay. Most, but not all, of the natural gas we use today comes from organisms that died millions of years ago. Their rotting remains fell to the bottom of lakes and oceans where they were buried under layers of sand and mud. As this sediment turned to stone, the gases released from the decaying material were trapped underground. The gases were caught in porous rocks as water is held in a sponge, up to 10 km (6 miles) under ground. More than a billion tonnes (tons) of natural gas are mined from sites all around the world every year.

GAS

• Methane gas produced under the piles of garbage at the Staten Island landfill is piped directly into the homes of thousands of New Yorkers who use it for cooking and for heating their homes. Plants and animals are always dying, so new supplies of natural gas are always being made. Scientists hope that we will be able to utilize more of the energy released from decaying organic matter. This energy could someday supply 15 to 30 per cent of our needs, replacing petroleum-based fuels such as oil.

• Thousands of years ago, the Chinese used hollow bamboo stalks to pipe natural gas from place to place. Colonial Americans used hollow logs. Today, the network of steel pipes that carries natural gas throughout Canada and the United States is long enough to circle the Earth 40 times! The largest pipes in the pipeline may be a metre (yard) wide. Gases under 75 atmospheres of pressure rush through them at up to 80 km/h (50 miles per hour). (One atmosphere of pressure is the normal pressure of the air around us.) Smaller pipes lead directly into people's homes and businesses.

• Natural gas is odourless, so a chemical is added to make it smell bad. Why? The smelly chemical is added to warn people if there is a gas leak. Leaking gas could cause a fire or an explosion. What should you do if you smell gas? Open the doors and windows and call the gas company from a neighbour's house. But remember, you're not really smelling gas at all. The disagreeable odour comes from mercaptan, a compound similar to the one that gives garlic its smell.

It's a Gas! **37**

The Earth's atmosphere

What is in the air around us? Some solid things such as birds, airplanes and all sorts of dust. Some liquid things such as drops of rain. And lots and lots of gases.

The air is a mixture of gases — mostly nitrogen and oxygen — with small amounts of other gases. This mixture changes from time to time — between day and night, for example, or between summer and winter. And it changes from place to place — from city to country, or from one altitude to another. What's in an *average* lungful of the air you breathe?

UNMIXING A MIXTURE

How do we know what gases are in the atmosphere? How can one invisible gas be separated from the rest of the mixture to measure it? Different chemicals change from liquids to gases at different temperatures. This gives chemists an easy way of "unmixing" the air.

The air is turned into a liquid by making it very, very cold. Then the temperature is allowed to rise again slowly. One by one, the different chemicals change back from liquids to

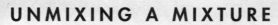

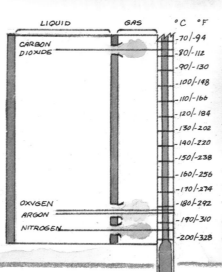

	LIQUID	GAS	°C	°F
CARBON DIOXIDE			-70	-94
			-80	-112
			-90	-130
			-100	-148
			-110	-166
			-120	-184
			-130	-202
			-140	-220
			-150	-238
			-160	-256
			-170	-274
OXYGEN			-180	-292
ARGON			-190	-310
NITROGEN			-200	-328

gases. Nitrogen goes first; it boils (evaporates) at -195°C (-319°F). Argon and oxygen follow at -185°C (-301°F) and -183°C (-297°F). But carbon dioxide has to be warmed all the way up to -78°C (-108°F) before it becomes a gas again. As each gas is released, scientists remove and measure it. By doing this, they are able to determine which gases, and how much of them, are present in the atmosphere.

What's in the air? Nitrogen

Nitrogen is the most plentiful gas in the air. It makes up more than three-quarters of the atmosphere — nearly 80 per cent. There are about 4000 billion tonnes (tons) of nitrogen gas in the air around the Earth, but most of it is just hanging there, doing nothing. As a gas, nitrogen isn't very active. It doesn't take part in chemical combinations very easily. So although we take in large amounts of nitrogen with every breath, we breathe it out again unchanged.

Could we live without nitrogen? No! Nitrogen is an essential part of proteins and amino acids, which are the building blocks of living things. But we can't get the nitrogen we need from the air. Instead, we get it from the foods we eat, thanks to tiny bacteria. These bacteria take nitrogen gas from air pockets in the soil and turn it into nitrogen compounds that plants can use. When you eat these plants, or the animals that have eaten them, you get the nitrogen that your body needs.

Processing plants

Nitrogen-fixing bacteria attach themselves to the roots of plants belonging to the legume family, which includes clover, soy beans and peas. Since clover is a pretty common weed, you can see for yourself.

You'll need:
- a clover plant from a lawn, field or roadside
- a digging tool
- water
- a small flat dish

1. Find a clover plant. (If you find a four-leaf clover, save the leaves and press them between the pages of a book. They're supposed to bring you good luck.)

2. Dig the plant up carefully, taking care not to damage its roots.

3. Shake off most of the soil and gently rinse the roots with water.

4. Place the plant on the dish and keep it moist. Look for nodules, which are little lumps on the fine hair-like roots branching from the thicker main root. Even without a magnifying glass, you will be able to see where the nitrogen-fixing bacteria live.

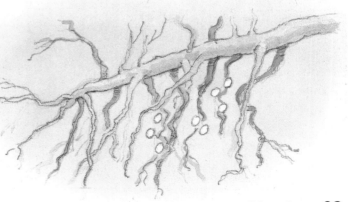

What's in the air? Oxygen

The next most plentiful gas in the atmosphere is oxygen. It makes up about 21 per cent of the air around us. Most animals need oxygen, whether they take it from the air as you do or from the water as a fish does.

Oxygen is a great combiner. Unlike nitrogen gas, oxygen combines easily with many other things. Sometimes the chemical combination, or oxidation, takes place very quickly, releasing lots of energy as heat and light. A fire burning is a good example of rapid oxidation. Sometimes oxidation takes place quite slowly. Your cells use oxygen to help "burn"

the food you eat, supplying your body with the energy it needs. This controlled, step-by-step process is a form of oxidation, too. Paint drying, a dead tree stump rotting, food spoiling, metals tarnishing and rusting are all changes that take place as the molecules in these things combine with the oxygen in the air.

When oxygen combines with another chemical element, compounds called oxides are formed. Oxides can be liquids such as water, solids such as rust, or gases such as carbon dioxide. Oxides are very common — and very plentiful. Did you know that water is hydrogen oxide? Every water molecule consists of two hydrogen molecules combined with an oxygen molecule. About half of the Earth's crust consists of rocks and minerals that are oxides, too. Most of the oxygen on the Earth is not found in the air as a gas; it's found in oxides and other chemical compounds.

Oxygen combines so easily with so many other chemicals that it's surprising that there is as much oxygen gas in the atmosphere as there is. Fortunately, oxygen is continually being recycled by green plants. During a process called photosynthesis, green plants use water, carbon dioxide and the energy of the sun to produce food. As this happens, water molecules, which are made up of hydrogen and oxygen atoms, are broken apart. Oxygen is released into the air again as a gas.

KILLER OXYGEN

Billions of years ago, the Earth's atmosphere wasn't made up of the same gases as it is today. It consisted mainly of ammonia and methane, gases that would be poisonous to you. There was hardly any oxygen gas. For the tiny blue-green algae and bacteria that  lived then, the atmosphere was perfect. They didn't need oxygen. In fact, the oxygen that they produced during photosynthesis was just a toxic waste — a poison! After hundreds of millions of years, enough oxygen gas had accumulated in the atmosphere to endanger the kinds of organisms that were producing it. Fortunately, other forms of life had been evolving, too, and some of these organisms flourished in the oxygen-polluted air. Today, most species of plants and animals depend on oxygen for survival.

Oxygen gas is still a poison for some bacteria today just as it was for ancient bacteria that lived millions of years ago. This makes oxygen useful as an antiseptic. Take the Band-aid off a cut as soon as possible. The oxygen in the air will help to kill bacteria on your skin that could cause an infection.

Too much oxygen gas can also be dangerous for human beings. During the 1940s, doctors were puzzled by the high rate of blindness among children who had been born prema-turely. These children were often placed in incubators for the first few weeks after birth. The mystery was solved when doctors realized that infants were being harmed by one of the gases pumped into their incubators — oxygen. Too much oxygen can damage the tiny capillaries of the lungs and bronchial tubes, or harm the capillaries in a tiny baby's eyes.

What's in the air? The noble gases

Together, nitrogen and oxygen gas make up about 99 per cent of the Earth's atmosphere. Traces of other gases make up the remainder. Six of these gases come from a special family called the noble gases. Gases in this family will not combine with other chemicals, even oxygen. The noble gases are also called the inert gases.

Argon is the most plentiful of the noble gases. It gets its name from the Greek word *argos*, which means lazy! Other gases in the family have Greek names, too. Krypton gets its name from the word *kryptos*, meaning hidden. Xenon comes from *xenos*, a word that means strange. Neon, the gas that's used in neon lights, means new. Radon, a radioactive gas, gets its name from radium, the mineral from which it is formed. Helium, which is seven times lighter than air, is named for *helios*, the Greek word for the sun. Helium was detected in the sun's atmosphere before it was found on Earth.

SAFETY FIRST

Hydrogen is the lightest gas there is. Why isn't it used to fill blimps, dirigibles and other airships instead of helium, which is heavier?

It used to be. But unlike helium, hydrogen gas is highly flammable and explosive. In 1937, a hydrogen-filled dirigible called the *Hindenburg* caught fire as it was landing in New Jersey after a trans-Atlantic flight. The hydrogen exploded, destroying the *Hindenburg* in less than two minutes and killing 34 people. This disaster, only one of many airship accidents, led people to look for a safer lighter-than-air gas to use instead of hydrogen. Helium was the answer.

How many helium balloons would it take to lift an average fourth-grader into the air? (Let's say that she weighs 34 kg [75 pounds].) Answer on page 62.

Answer on page 62.

It's a Gas! **43**

What's in the air? Carbon dioxide

Although there's only a tiny amount in Earth's atmosphere — about ³⁄₁₀₀ of one per cent — carbon dioxide is a very important gas. It is the gas that many animals exchange with plants for the oxygen they need to stay alive. Animals release carbon dioxide when they exhale. Green plants use the carbon dioxide during photosynthesis and return oxygen gas to the air. Carbon dioxide is also released from wood, coal and other fuels as they burn, and from the remains of plants and animals as they decay.

Animals use oxygen and give off carbon dioxide.

Plants use carbon dioxide and give off oxygen.

DID YOU KNOW?

Without carbon dioxide, human beings wouldn't be able to breathe. It is the build-up of carbon dioxide in your blood, not just a lack of oxygen, that tells your brain you need to take another breath.

Carbon dioxide and other greenhouse gases trap the sun's heat.

Three-one-hundredths of one per cent is about the right amount of carbon dioxide for life on Earth today. Without that little bit of carbon dioxide in the atmosphere, some scientists think the Earth would be so cold that the oceans would freeze. Why? Carbon dioxide is one of the "greenhouse" gases. Greenhouse gases in the Earth's atmosphere act like the glass windows in a greenhouse. Light from the sun can pass in through these barriers, but heat is unable to pass back out.

Over the last 200 years, the amount of carbon dioxide in the atmosphere has been rising. Scientists are worried that the extra carbon dioxide will keep too much heat trapped inside the Earth's atmosphere. As a result, the planet may be overheating.

Where is the extra carbon dioxide coming from? It comes from people — not from the small amounts that we breathe out, but from the fuels we burn. Every North American contributes about five tonnes (tons) of carbon dioxide gas to the overloaded atmosphere every year as we drive our cars, heat our houses and run our factories. At the same time, the green plants that use up carbon dioxide during photosynthesis are being destroyed; forests are cut down for lumber and paper, or cleared to make room for the grazing of cattle.

Build a model greenhouse

A sheet of glass lets light pass into a greenhouse but prevents heat from escaping. Try this activity to see what a good heat-trap a greenhouse can be. The greenhouse gases, including carbon dioxide, trap heat in a similar way.

You'll need:
- a pane of double-thickness window glass, large enough to cover one of the pans
- masking tape
- 2 pans, each about 23 x 33 cm (9 x 13 inches)
- soil
- 2 small wooden blocks or boxes
- 3 weather thermometers (fever thermometers won't work)

1. Ask an adult to carefully cover all four edges of the sheet of glass with a protective layer of masking tape.

2. Wait until noon on a hot, sunny day to do this experiment. Put a layer of dirt about 2 cm (1 inch) deep in each of the two pans. Rest a thermometer on a wooden block or small box in each pan as shown. Cover one of the boxes with your sheet of glass. Set the two pans in the sun. Place the third thermometer nearby in the shade.

3. Leave the two pans out in the full sun for at least 20 minutes, then compare the temperature on the two thermometers in the pans. Which one is higher — the temperature in the open pan or the temperature in the greenhouse? What is the temperature in the shade?

What else is in the air? Air pollution

Carbon dioxide is not the only polluting gas that comes pouring out of chimneys, smokestacks and tailpipes. And the greenhouse effect is not the only thing that has environmentalists worried. City smog, acid rain and holes in the ozone layer are other major problems that are caused by a growing human population.

Smog is a word that was made up to describe the dirty air that hangs over big cities and industrial areas. It's a combination of two other words — smoke and fog. There are two main types of smog. Where the climate is damp — in European cities, for example, or along the eastern seaboard of the United States — the smog contains harmful sulphur compounds. In the early 1900s, sulphurous smog from the coal-burning fires of London, Glasgow and Edinburgh killed thousands of people.

Where the climate is hot and sunny — in Los Angeles, for example — a different type of smog is common, an ozone smog. Ozone gas is formed by the interaction of bright sunlight with the exhaust fumes from automobiles and factories. Ozone is a dangerous pollutant when it's found at ground level, although it's an essential part of the upper atmosphere.

Acid rain is the result of acidic fumes that form when fossil fuels, such as coal, oil and gasoline, are burned. Gases such as sulphur dioxide and nitrous dioxide dissolve in the water vapour in clouds, turning into sulphuric and nitric acids. When the water vapour condenses into rain, the rain is acidic, too. Wherever it falls, acid rain makes water in the soil, lakes and rivers acidic, killing plants and animals. Because the damaging fumes are carried away by the wind, acid rain has damaged forests and farmlands far away from the areas where the pollution began. Many countries now have laws that require factories to filter their fumes to remove acidic chemicals before they release them into the atmosphere.

The ozone layer is a belt of ozone gas that floats in the upper part of the Earth's atmosphere. This layer is essential to life on Earth because it is the only gas in the outer atmosphere that can block out certain dangerous parts of the sun's radiation. In the spring of 1985, a gigantic hole was discovered in the ozone layer over Antarctica. The hole was larger than the United States and deeper than Mount Everest. Since then, the problem has become worse.

What's causing the destruction of the ozone layer? Many industrial chemicals are released into the atmosphere. When they float up to the ozone layer, new chemicals are formed that attack and destroy the ozone.

DID YOU KNOW?

People in California use enough spray-on cosmetics, such as antiperspirants, hairspray and shaving cream, to add 27 tonnes (tons) of hazardous gases to the air *every day*! According to the California Air Resources Board, a single can of spray-on deodorant releases the same amount of polluting hydrocarbons that a car does on a 1200-km (746-mile) drive.

GETTING TO THE OZONE LAYER

If you could drive a car straight up into the sky, how long do you think it would take you to drive to the ozone layer, the outer edge of the Earth's atmosphere? If you drove at a normal highway speed, you would get there in less than half an hour! The Earth's atmosphere is only about 40 km (25 miles) thick.

Have you ever taken off in an airplane on a cloudy, rainy day? After a few minutes of climbing through the clouds, the airplane breaks through, leaving the rain below. Half of Earth's atmosphere (and most of its weather) lies within 5.6 km (3½ miles) of the ground. As the airplane climbs, the air gets thinner and thinner. Why? The atmosphere is tied to the Earth by the force of gravity. As you fly farther from the Earth, the gravitational pull (the pull of gravity) gets weaker and gases start to escape. Without gravity to hold it down, the atmosphere would float out into space.

DID YOU KNOW?

• The gravitational pull of the sun and moon creates tides in the atmosphere as well as in the oceans. Twice a day, as the Earth turns on its axis, there will be a rise and fall in the atmospheric pressure at any given place. Why? The side of the Earth closest to the sun or the moon experiences a greater gravitational attraction than the side of the Earth facing away. The gravitational pull creates a high tide.

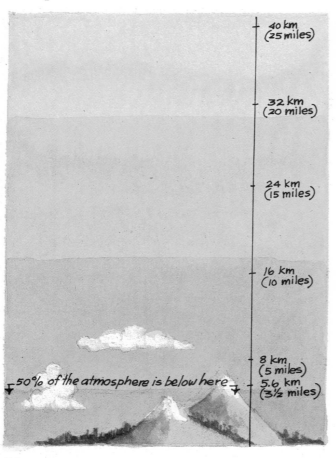

40 km (25 miles)

32 km (20 miles)

24 km (15 miles)

16 km (10 miles)

8 km (5 miles)

5.6 km (3½ miles)

50% of the atmosphere is below here

• Only hydrogen gas is light enough to escape the Earth's gravitational pull. Although hydrogen is the most plentiful element in the universe, only a trace of hydrogen gas is found in the Earth's atmosphere. Most of the hydrogen is found in outer space. In interplanetary space — the space between the planets — there are about 30 molecules of hydrogen per cubic centimetre (490 molecules per cubic inch). In interstellar space, which is beyond our solar system, there are approximately ten molecules per cubic centimetre (164 molecules per cubic inch). Even in intergalactic space, which is between the galaxies, astronomers estimate that there is still a single molecule of hydrogen in a cubic centimetre of space (or 16 molecules in a cubic inch).

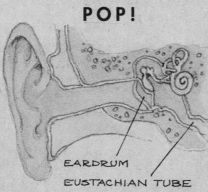

POP!

EARDRUM
EUSTACHIAN TUBE

Have you ever felt your ears "pop" as you were taking off in an airplane? The popping sensation is caused by changes in the air pressure as the airplane moves higher and higher — and the air gets thinner and thinner. Even though the cabin of the plane is pressurized for the safety and comfort of everyone on board, the pressure inside the plane at cruising altitudes is usually not quite as high as it was on the ground.

Why do your ears feel the change? Your ears are connected to the inside of your throat by your Eustachian tubes. When you're still on the ground, the air pressure is the same on both sides of your eardrum. It's the same inside your throat as it is outside in the air around you. But as the plane climbs higher, the air pressure in the cabin starts to fall. Now the air pressure inside your ear is greater than the air pressure outside, and it presses uncomfortably against your eardrum. Opening your mouth helps to equalize the pressure again, so some people recommend chewing gum during take-offs and landings.

Other atmospheres

There are nine planets in our solar system. Some of these planets, including Earth, have gaseous atmospheres. Others have no atmosphere at all. Some planets are almost all atmosphere — their cores are small compared to the enormously thick layers of gases that surround them.

Astronomers usually divide the planets into two groups. The inner planets (Mercury, Venus, Earth and Mars) are small dense planets, largely made of rocks and metals. They're called the terrestrial (Earth-like) planets. The outer plants (Jupiter, Saturn, Uranus and Neptune) are called the gas giants. These four planets are composed largely of gases such as hydrogen, helium, methane and ammonia. And they really are giants. Uranus, the smallest, has a diameter that's three times as big as Earth's. Jupiter, the largest, has a diameter 11 times as big.

Pluto, the ninth planet, doesn't fit into either group. Some scientists think Pluto isn't a planet at all, just a piece of a moon that escaped from the orbit of Neptune.

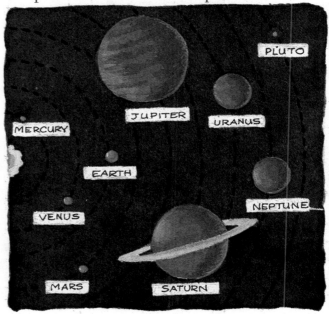

MERCURY
JUPITER
PLUTO
URANUS
EARTH
VENUS
NEPTUNE
MARS
SATURN

Which planet is which?

Can you match each planet with the correct description? Answers on page 62.

1. This planet has no atmosphere at all. All the gases have escaped out into space because of the planet's intense heat and weak gravitational pull. This planet is small and very close to the sun.

2. These two giant planets are so far away from the sun that it's hard to see them, even with a telescope. They appear to be a pale bluish-green because of the methane gas in their upper atmospheres.

3. This planet's atmosphere is made up mostly of lighter gases such as hydrogen and helium. One of its ten moons, Titan, is large enough to have an atmosphere of its own. This planet is famous for its rings.

4. This tiny distant planet is too cold to have an atmosphere. At -200°C (-328°F), any gases around it would freeze.

5. This planet has an atmosphere that is 97 per cent carbon dioxide. This causes a greenhouse effect that heats up the surface to 482°C (900°F), even at night. This planet is almost the same size as Earth.

6. This planet's atmosphere is mostly nitrogen, oxygen and carbon dioxide gases. It is the only planet where liquid water can be found.

7. The atmosphere of this giant planet, which is composed mostly of hydrogen and helium gases, may be as much as 1000 km (625 miles) thick. Astronomers think this planet's Great Red Spot may be a giant storm in the upper atmosphere. And what a storm! It's 40 000 km (25 000 miles) across, and it has already lasted at least 300 years!

8. Ice covers the poles of this reddish planet, but it's not frozen water. It's frozen carbon dioxide — the main gas in this planet's atmosphere.

DID YOU KNOW?

• The planet Saturn is lighter than many types of wood. It would float — if you could find a large enough ocean! Like the other gas giants, Saturn is largely composed of the very light gases: hydrogen, helium, methane and ammonia.

• A star begins as a huge cloud of gas — mostly hydrogen — pulled together by the force of gravity. The cloud's gravitational field pulls in more and more gases and particles of dust until the cloud collapses into a hot, dense ball. Gravity continues to pack this *protostar* more and more tightly together, and the temperature at the core steadily rises. The core starts to glow. At 10 000 000°C (18 000 000°F) and under enormous pressure, the core reaches the point where hydrogen is turned into helium. The star's thermonuclear furnace is lit. Heat and light generated in the core burst to the surface. A shining star is born!

Gases in action

Have you ever seen a gas? Probably not. Most of the gases in the air around you are invisible. Luckily, there are other ways to observe the colourless, tasteless and odourless gases all around us. You can see — and feel — gases in action, even if you can't see the gases themselves. Try these activities and have fun watching how gases behave.

Seeing is believing

When is an invisible gas easy to see? When it's a bubble! A bubble is just gas surrounded by a liquid skin. Mixing baking soda and vinegar together is a good way to make a lot of carbon dioxide gas in a hurry. The gas will bubble right out of the container if you're not careful. Here's a way to slow the process down, so you can get a better look.

You'll need:
- 5 mL (1 tsp) baking soda
- 2 tall, skinny glasses or clear bottles
- cooking oil
- 30 mL (2 tbsp) vinegar
- food colouring

1. Put the baking soda in the bottom of one of the glasses and cover it with a layer of cooking oil about 2.5 cm (1 inch) deep. Any bubbles yet? Baking soda will not react with oil because oil is not acidic.

2. Mix the vinegar with a couple of drops of food colouring in the other glass.

3. Add the coloured vinegar slowly to the first glass, a few drops at a time. The vinegar will sink below the oil and react with the baking soda underneath. The bubbles of carbon dioxide gas that form have to work their way up slowly through the thick oil, giving you enough time to take a closer look. When the reaction slows down or stops, add a few more drops of vinegar. As long as you see baking soda on the bottom of the glass, you can make the bubbling start up again.

Puddle races

Have you ever watched a pot of water boiling on the stove, or seen laundry hung up on the clothes-line to dry? Have you ever fogged up a window or mirror with your breath, or seen your breath outdoors on a cold winter day? These are everyday examples of gases in action. When you watch water boiling or evaporating, you're seeing a liquid turning into a gas. When your breath forms a cloud, you're seeing a water vapour — a gas — condensing into a liquid again.

How fast can you make a puddle of water evaporate into a gas? Have a race with some of your friends and see!

You'll need:
- clean water
- washable markers or chalk
- a smooth, waterproof counter or table
- newspapers
- goose-necked lamps (if available)

1. Choose someone to act as a timekeeper or referee.

2. Each contestant starts by putting a small puddle of water on the counter or table-top. You don't need much water. Five small drops are fine for a short race.

3. Draw an outline around each puddle with a washable marker or a piece of chalk.

4. When the referee yells, "Let the best puddle win!" contestants try to help their puddles dry as fast as possible. Puddles may be blown on, fanned with a newspaper, warmed by a light bulb and so on, but no one can touch the puddles. The first contestant to make his or her puddle disappear completely is the winner!

PUDDLE RACE RECORD

Can you beat this record set by children at the Willingdon School in Montreal in 1992? Using a small hairdryer, they made 1mL (¼ tsp) of water evaporate in 7 minutes and 13 seconds. Under a teacher's supervision, the same kids tried another race, using laboratory alcohol instead of water. They were able to make 1 mL (¼ tsp) of lab alcohol vanish in just 1 minute and 9 seconds. Alcohol was fun to try because it evaporated *faster* than water. Can you think of any liquids that evaporate more *slowly* than water?

BRRRRRRRR!

Water can turn from a solid to a gas without ever having to be a liquid. Wet a handkerchief, wring it out well and spread it out in your freezer. In a couple of hours, it will have become stiff as the water freezes. If you come back a couple of days later, however, something surprising will have happened. The handkerchief will be soft and pliable again. The ice has evaporated directly into water vapour. If you hang your laundry out on the clothes-line at -25°C (-13°F), your neighbours might think you're weird, but your clothes will eventually dry. It will just take longer than it would on a hot summer day.

Secret messages

Dear Mom: Hope you saved some hot water for me!

You can leave a secret message for the next person who takes a hot bath or shower at your house. How? By turning an invisible gas into a visible liquid! Clean and dry the bathroom mirror carefully before you start. Then write your message on the glass with a tiny drop of dishwashing liquid dabbed on the tip of your finger. Your message will be invisible until the bathroom mirror steams up. As droplets from the steamy water vapour condense on the colder glass, your message will suddenly appear.

Why do the soapy areas stay clear? If you touch the writing, you'll feel that the mirror is wet there, too. The difference is that the soap allows the water to form a thin and transparent film instead of the cloudy droplets that cover the rest of the mirror.

Kitchen science

Your kitchen is a good place to find gases at work. Check out the things you eat and drink and take a lesson in gases from the bubbliest thing in your fridge — a soft drink!

You'll need:
- 1 very cold soft drink in a bottle with a pry-off or twist-off cap
- a bottle opener (if necessary)

Put the cold bottle in front of you and quickly lift or twist off the cap. What do you see inside the neck of the bottle right after you open it? The bottle did not have that cloud of mist inside it before it was opened. Where did the cloud come from? Enjoy your drink while you read about the answer to this mystery.

The fizz in your drink — carbon dioxide gas — is pumped into the liquid just before the cap is put on the bottle. Most of the gas forms bubbles that are dissolved in the liquid. However, some carbon dioxide gas and water vapour remain in the neck of the bottle until the cap is removed.

What happens when you open the bottle? The gases and vapours that were trapped under pressure rush out. As the pressure suddenly drops, so does the temperature inside the neck of the bottle. The water vapour condenses back into water droplets and forms the cloud that you see.

What usually happens when you open a *warm* drink? You have to be careful or it might overflow. Why? The drink was very cold when the carbon dioxide gas was originally pumped into it at the bottling plant. If the drink gets warm, the liquid can't hold as much dissolved gas. More of the gas is trapped in the neck of the bottle. It escapes from the neck of the bottle faster and more dramatically than it does from the liquid. Can you figure out why soft drinks bubble over if they're shaken before being opened?

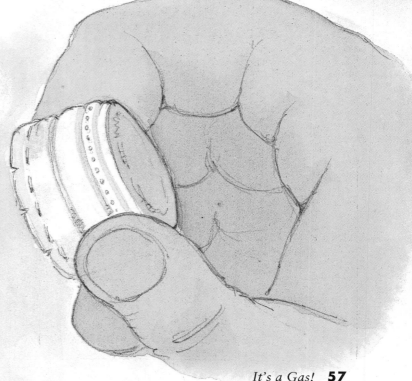

More fun with fizz

You've heard about carbonated drinks, but what about carbonated candy? Have you ever tried the powdery candy that fizzes and crackles when you put it in your mouth? You can make it at home with this recipe.

You'll need:
- 20 mL (1½ tbsp) citric acid (available at a drugstore)
- 2 mL (½ tsp) baking soda
- 30 mL (2 tbsp) granulated sugar
- flavoured drink or gelatin crystals (optional)

Mix the citric acid, baking soda and sugar together. If you like a sour taste, put some of this mixture in the palm of your hand and take a little lick. If it's too sour, add more sugar and 30 mL (2 tbsp) of flavoured drink or gelatin crystals for flavouring.

When the citric acid crystals become wet in your mouth, they form an acid that reacts with the baking soda to produce carbon dioxide gas.

DANCING DROPS

The next time an adult is planning to cook something in a frying pan, ask him to sprinkle a few drops of water into the hot, empty pan. The water droplets will hop and skitter around in the pan for a surprisingly long time before they evaporate. Why? When the drop first touches the hot surface, the bottom of it immediately turns into a gas, separating the rest of the drop from the heat. The watery portion of the drop dances around, supported by the layer of vapour just as a hovercraft moves across the surface of the water. Only when enough heat has been transferred to the rest of the drop will the water evaporate completely.

Rust

The oxygen in the air you breathe is essential for keeping you alive. The same gas is responsible for a common household problem — rust. Try this experiment to see how oxygen is taken out of the air by metal as it rusts.

You'll need:

- a large flat pan
- water
- food colouring
- a small glass
- a clean new pad of steel wool
- a large clear jar

1. Fill the pan halfway with water and add a bit of food colouring. Lower the glass into the pan, upside down and at an angle, so that it too has water in it.

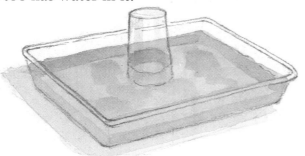

2. Wet the steel wool, shaking off any excess water, and put it on top of the upside-down glass. Cover the steel wool and the glass with the large clear jar. The rim of the jar should be completely under water.

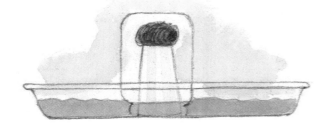

3. Leave the experiment undisturbed until you can see that the steel wool has started to rust. Compare the water level in the pan with the water level in the upside-down jar. What causes the water levels to change? As the steel wool rusts, it uses up some of the oxygen under the jar. The water rises to take its place.

If you have a scale that can measure small weights accurately, try weighing the piece of steel wool before and after the experiment. The steel wool should be heavier after it has rusted. Why? Oxygen molecules combine with the metal in the steel wool, adding extra weight.

Pressure power

Have you ever sucked a drink up a straw? If you answered yes, think again. You don't suck the drink up the straw. Something *pushes* it up — the pressure of the gases in the air around you. When you suck on the end of a straw, you reduce the air pressure inside the tube. The pressure of the air pushing down on the surface of the liquid in the glass is greater. It forces the drink up through the straw.

The air pressure around you is greater than you might think. Surprise yourself and your friends with this activity.

You'll need:
• a plastic foam cup
• water
• a small sheet of writing paper
• a sink

1. Fill the plastic foam cup completely with water. The surface of the water will bulge up over the rim of the cup.
2. Cut a square of paper big enough

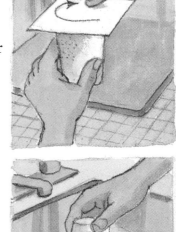

to cover the opening of the cup. Hold the cup over a sink. Carefully lower the paper onto the surface of the water. Gently rub your finger around the rim of the cup. A little water will spill as you press the paper down.

3. Hold the cup with the paper cover over the sink and turn it upside down. How can a flimsy piece of paper hold up the water in the cup? The force of the air pushing up on the paper is greater than the weight of the water pressing down.

4. Try the experiment again but this time fill the cup only three-quarters full. (Remember to hold the cup and paper over the sink.) What do you think will happen this time?

DID YOU KNOW?
A water pistol wouldn't work on the moon. As you pump the trigger, air is pulled into the gun, compressed and used to force a spray of water out the nozzle. Since the moon has no atmosphere, there's no air — or air pressure — to make the gun squirt.

Can you stab a drinking straw through a raw potato with a single jab? "There must be a trick," you're thinking, and you're right.

Test your strength!

Cover one end of the straw with a finger as you plunge it into the potato. The air trapped inside will make the straw rigid enough, and strong enough, to go right through the potato.

ANSWERS

Who am I?, page 16

A frog. As a tadpole, the frog breathes through gills. As an adult, the frog breathes with lungs. Buried, inactive, in the mud at the bottom of a pond all winter, it gets enough oxygen from the water through its very thin skin.

Helium balloons, page 43

About 6000, depending on the size of the balloons and the weather conditions. Each balloon has to lift its own weight plus its share of the weight of the strings. There's not much lifting power left over for the student.

Which planet is which?, page 52

1. Mercury 2. Uranus and Neptune
3. Saturn 4. Pluto 5. Venus 6. Earth
7. Jupiter 8. Mars

GLOSSARY

Air: The mixture of gases that surrounds us. Dry air is made up of nitrogen (78%), oxygen (21%), carbon dioxide (less than 1%) and traces of other gases.

Altitude: The height of an object above sea level

Atmosphere: The layer of gases that surrounds a planet

Atom: The smallest amount of an element that can exist. Atoms are like the littlest building blocks in a set. They combine to form molecules and other larger structures.

Cell: The microscopic building block of living things. Some organisms consist of a single cell, but most plants and animals contain many different types of cells. These cells combine to form different kinds of tissues and organs.

Chemistry: The science of elements and compounds. Chemists study the ways in which atoms and molecules combine.

Combustion: The rapid oxidation of a fuel to produce heat and light

Compound: A substance made up of two or more elements. Water is a compound made up of hydrogen and oxygen atoms.

Condensation: The change from a gaseous state to a liquid state

Element: A substance that consists of a single kind of atom. An element can't be separated into a simpler substance. There are fewer than 100 naturally occurring elements.

Evaporation: The change from a liquid state to a gaseous state as molecules escape from the surface of a liquid. Boiling is one form of evaporation.

Gas: One of the three states of matter (the other two states are liquid and solid). A gas can expand indefinitely and has no definite shape or size.

Inert gases: A family of gases (also called the noble gases) that rarely form chemical compounds

Liquid: One of the three states of matter (the other two states are solid and gas). A liquid changes shape depending on the container it's in, but a liquid has a definite volume that doesn't change. Unlike gases, liquids cannot be compressed.

Mass: The amount of matter in an object, measured in grams and kilograms. Mass is different from weight, which is also measured in these units. The weight of an object changes depending on the strength of the gravitational pull acting on it; the mass of an object stays the same. An astronaut weighs less on the moon than on Earth because the moon's gravitational pull is weaker than the Earth's.

Molecule: A group of atoms held together by chemical bonds. A carbon dioxide molecule, for example, consists of a carbon atom attached to two oxygen atoms. Some molecules contain thousands of atoms. Other molecules consist of a single atom.

Organism: A living thing

Oxidation: A chemical reaction involving oxygen

Photosynthesis: The chemical process by which green plants combine carbon dioxide and water into food molecules, using the energy of sunlight. Photosynthesis is the foundation of the entire food chain because most animals depend on green plants, directly or indirectly, for food.

Pressure: A force exerted continuously on one thing by another thing. In gases, pressure is exerted in all directions.

Solid: One of the three states of matter (the other two are liquid and gas). A solid consists of molecules packed closely together, arranged in a fixed, orderly pattern. A solid does not change shape or size unless a force is applied.

INDEX